MW00438528

Identity Theft

Identity Theft

Joseph Harrison

WAYWISER

First published in 2008 by

THE WAYWISER PRESS

14 Lyncroft Gardens, Ewell, Surrey KT17 1UR, UK
P.O. Box 6205, Baltimore, MD 21206, USA
www.waywiser-press.com

Managing Editor
Philip Hoy

Associate Editors
Joseph Harrison   Clive Watkins   Greg Williamson

Hardback ISBN
978-1-904130-29-1

Paperback ISBN
978-1-904130-27-7

Printed and bound by
Cromwell Press Ltd., Trowbridge, Wiltshire

for Carla

Acknowledgements

The author would like to thank the editors of the magazines in which some of some of these poems first appeared: *Raritan*: "Touch and Go," "Paper View," "Nautical Terms"; *Sewanee Theological Review*: "Gum," "Identity Theft"; *The Sewanee Review*: "For Anthony Hecht"; *Smartish Pace*: "To False Spring," "To a House Sparrow," "To the Wind", "The Catch"; *Southern Humanities Review*: "Who They Were"; *Southwest Review*: "For Donald Justice"; *The Yale Review*: "To An Aldabran Tortoise, Dead at 250."

Contents

I   Trajectories

II   Odes and Elegies

III   Tropes

Contents

IV   Odes

I Trajectories

The Catch

Scientists recently announced that huge Asian big head carp are on their way to the Great Lakes. The fish are known for jumping into fishermen's boats, often causing injury. – *The Washington Post*

After some twenty-odd years
    In dubious boats
    ("You call *that* a craft?")
("Well, sometimes it kind of floats"),

With hand-me-down, broken tackle,
    Vanishing bait,
    And a boredom only
Sleep can alleviate,

As patience keeps coming up empty
    Like a snapped line
    ("Though this is all
I have, it isn't mine"),

When fish are merely theory
    And hunger a fact,
    And not a thing
Worth eating gets caught in the act

But the odd compliment,
    Not what you fish for,
    Till wishing your wishing
Would end is all you wish for,

Out of the blue comes news
    Of aquatic confusion
    And piscatory
Peril from the intrusion

The Catch

Into our longest rivers
    And largest lakes,
    Occasioning
Slack jaws and double takes,

Plus bruises, cuts, and pains
    Both dull and sharp,
    Of strange, colossal
Asian big head carp

That grow to sixty pounds
    And four feet plus,
    And as if impelled
By compulsion to concuss

Jump ten feet in the air
    And, willy-nilly,
    Crash land in boats,
Knocking the fishermen silly,

As if we weren't so already,
    Setting out
    In quest of triumphs
Brief as a waterspout

And rarely as substantial,
    Often consisting
    Of great improbable
Trophies we keep insisting

We actually almost landed
    One fine day
    (The luring headline:
HUGE FISH GETS AWAY),

Until such whoppers seem
    The whole intent
    Of annals of
Piscine endeavorment

And we drift, careless, breezy
    ("What's that bumpin'?")
    ("Maybe a big one,
Eh? Let's hope they're jumpin'") ...

Better reel in the line
    And batten the hatch.
    You finally got
What you asked for. That's the catch.

Identity Theft

The perils of our hyperdigital age
Hover in microrealms of cyberspace,
Waiting to disappear the vanished page
(What brief felicities fell out of place,
What midnight labors lost to lose the case!)
You (expletive!) *deleted,* zapped to square
Zero, cut past retrieval, launched into space
Blacker than black holes, thinner than thin air,
A technoillogic anti-world that isn't there.

Now all our information circulates
Through networks, camouflaged and limacine,
That monitor accounts and payment dates
And know just what we've bought, know where we've "been,"
And sell that information, site unseen,
To anyone pretending enterprise.
We're just a set of numbers on a screen,
Numbers that serve the purposes of lies
Inducing massive information compromise.

Some sly, pretexting phisher, who's expert
In legerdemain's most current digital cons
To siphon funds before a fraud alert,
Brandishes false security icons
And, deft as a neurosurgeon slicing pons,
Breaches our firewall, accessing our cache.
His toxic terms invade our lexicons,
Taxing our systems staggering toward a crash
But not before he's flowed our info into cash.

It seems that someone else has got your name
Where all identity is virtual
And masquerade is party to the game,
And as he plays your credit's in free fall.
The world his oyster, the false You's having a ball
In Punta Cana, Mexico, Brazil.
Where all is credit, some will credit all:
Aiming at your good name, with time to kill,
He's scripting your only move, he's virtually writing your will.

But who needed that identity, anyway?
Your very number's socially insecure,
And daily, faceless at the NSA
Behind black glass, empowered to secure
Security, they're spying, that's for sure,
Safe in their cubical polyopticon,
With satellite interception to insure
They're on our chatter as we chatter on,
All processed by the secret program Echelon.

So so long privacy, and any sense
Identity itself remains intact.
There's no such thing as virtual innocence.
Now everything's public, every public act
Is you, you're John Q. Public, since in fact
You line up like the next guy, you're just the same,
Same suit, same shoes, exactly the same contract,
The social one of inquisition, shame,
And punishment by numbers, lots. What's in a name?

(And your own name was always your father's, too,
The first you, and the bigger man as well,
Which made you number two, the second you.)
Names do have their intentions, they bluntly tell
Too little or too much. If Florimell –
No, let her wait. Say that your folks, in pride,
Decided Abraham Lincoln Graham Bell
Might augur greatness ... . Their friends were horrified,
The future much amused, and you, you wanted to hide.

For what's more arbitrary than a name?
Even "identity," that seminal term,
Derives from "*idem,*" which just means "the same."
But same as what? As whom? Confused, infirm,
The sense of self as core, essential germ
Emerging from the vast genetic scrum
Through coded interplay of egg and sperm
As someone really you, is overcome,
Cleaned up, sponged off, wiped out, stopped *in exordium.*

Identity itself becomes the thief
Stealing away with all we never had.
We've changed? Matured? Turned over a new leaf
In the volume of the self? Or slipped? Gone bad?
The epic of our lives, the ___ *iad,*
Has no one in it stable enough to change,
Whether the hero's Artegall or Chad:
No growth potential, no peak, no depth, no range.
It's all far too familiar, and then it's all too strange.

The person in the mirror isn't me,
He isn't anyone. Image is all
Or nothing. Now reality TV
Becomes our window on the world, the fall
Brings brand old characters, in what we call
Interesting situations: tension, strife,
Treachery, eating insects. It's comical,
Or would be if the spectacle weren't rife
With resonant hollowness, our need to get a life.

But if we had a life, what would we do?
There's freedom in not being anyone.
Pronominal confusion – "me" and "you,"
Like "us" and "them," are codependent, "one"
Must, nervous, glance at "many," as the son
Looks backward at the father – runs amok.
Though you *were* one of us, under the gun
We've joined them, and you are out of luck.
When asked our name (whose name?) in court, you stood, dumbstruck.

And what identity you have you stole.
That smile, that gesture, that quirky turn of phrase
Are just as patterned as the caracole
The rider learns to manage. All your days
You've been accumulating such displays
Of influence. It's easy enough to date
The habits of your practice, phase by phase.
You're hybrid, mongrel, patchwork, complicate,
A gallimaufry. Just be yourself? It's far too late.

You're no more you than you're a character
Lost in the labyrinth of *The Faerie Queene*.
"This path leads where? Why are there two of her?"
You've double Florimells to choose between:
The differences are huge, but can't be seen.
It's all a hall of mirrors, with no way out,
Endless. You multiply. Behind the screen,
Immeritô, E. K., and Colin Clout
Masked and unmasked, identity remains in doubt.

Scholars are fools by trade, but so's the poet
Whose narcissistic tale, which he must tell,
Rings full of echoes and he doesn't know it.
In seeking who you are, you might as well
Be one of the knights pursuing Florimell
Who, scared of everything, keeps running away,
Streaking by on her palfrey like a bat out of hell.
(The true one, that is; the false one's glad to stay.)
No, you can't win the game, and, yes, you have to play.

And Florimell's girdle, apogee of art
And echoing renown, self without end?
All the Old Masters have a big head start
And who are you? To what do *you* pretend?
Fasten your armor, chump, prepare to defend
Yourself against the champion, The Past.
Under enormous pressure you will bend
Then snap. The game will play you, hard and fast,
From your first tentative misstep to your tottering last.

Retired, you're shipped off to the Last Resort
Where the old losers linger, contemplating
What might have been. There's never a final report,
Just a slow, blurry fade-out, with everyone waiting
For nothing to stop happening. False You's dating
False Florimell, but no one heard the chimes
At midnight, once. Abe Lincoln Bell's berating
His cell phone; Artegall's up on war crimes;
Chad should be, too. Oh well. These are, or were, bad times.

Or you wander, at last, into the Cave of Despair,
The site the evil omens all portend:
The scattered corpses, the cries, the putrid air,
The smooth-talking assassin who's your friend.
You've broken more than you can ever mend
And debts are never cancelled. What's up? The game.
You know who's coming to get you in the end,
The ultimate thief who takes us all the same
And pockets every precious asset, even your name.

Virtual Death

A Korean man collapsed and died after playing a video game for 49 hours straight. It was one of several similar deaths over the last few years.

Let's not pretend we don't know how he felt,
The compulsion of obsession, pushing beyond
The limits of the body, because the mind,
Synapses firing and firing, can't let go.
The body's nothing, weak, its miserable needs –
A shift in posture, sleep, a little food –
Are nothing compared to adrenal presences
Like fear and joy unleashing their jolts, and now
You're hooked on this one, figuring the terrain,
Marking the dangers, starting to read the game,
And, yes, invested in your character
Whose life or death is really on the line
And matters, more than you know or want to know.

(The game is Starcraft, battle simulation
With multiplayer mayhem on the edge
Of the galaxy, intuitive interface
With hard-core gamers hundreds of miles away
Camped in the cybercafes and jacked to the skies,
Living on instant noodles and cigarettes,
Napping on fold-out cots, then back to action
Wired up, dialed in, locked on, and wary of movement:
Protoss, Zergs, and Terrans are on the prowl
As cracks in the Alliance begin to spread,
Dark Templars start appearing – what's *their* motive? –
And all beware Kerrigan, Queen of Blades ...)

A life on-line – with whose life on the line?
Somewhere a clock ticks, pressure takes its toll,
The body paying with every vital amp
Firing away. Let's not pretend, late night,
Light-headed, eyes fixed on the morphing screen
So long past quitting time time seems to stop,
When space shrinks to an artificial window
Where every swerve brings peril, joy, and fear
And on you battle, missing the hidden turn
Out of the labyrinth, missing the word
Sharp as a Saxon sword to slay the beast
Still howling for sacrifice, let's not pretend
We don't know how he felt, unable to stop.

Not even when a worried emissary
From your frantic mother reaches the cybercafe
Pleading with you to come home, get some rest,
Some decent food: but now the game is peaking,
In a blaze of spectral fire you live or die
And terminate your epic compulsive quest,
You've played the game, it's played you, and you're done,
You stagger to the bathroom, collapse on the floor
("Heart failure from exhaustion"), and really die
Where space is virtual but time is time.

Hikikomori

Japanese for "withdrawal," the term refers both to the condition of those people, usually young males, who retreat to their room and refuse to come out, sometimes for many years, and to those suffering from that condition, estimated by at least one expert to constitute 1% of the Japanese population.

Though the phenomenon is Japanese,
The impulse, to do precisely as you please,
Turning your back on social expectation,
Parental pressure, class humiliation,
And all the rapid brutal give and take,
More take than give both on and off the make,
Of going to and fro, from habit or need,
In this our world ramped up to hyperspeed
And taxing every jumpy nerve we've got
With information surfeit, polyglot
Configurations of whatever next
Installment of the social hypertext
Is paramount lest one be left behind
The swift proverbial curve and flounder, mind
Out of time times out of mind, is common to
The species. Since the whole thing's coming to
An interfacing universal mess
To end all messes in a vast distress
So intercalibrated we will all
Fall in a nanosecond of one fall
By someone lapsing somewhere (a butterfly's wings
Set off a chain reaction, and all things
Sink to sheer ruin and sudden misery,
As melting ice caps slide into the sea),
The social contract doesn't look so great.
You didn't want this. Why participate?
In cultures where there's nothing but the norm
And confident assumption you'll conform,
Without resort to clubs and cliques and clans
Like gangs and Goths and Young Republicans
To band together in an anti-style
Or posse up and angrily revile
The Bloods or Democrats, ready to do

Hikikomori

One in, without such dark companions, you
Are nothing but yourself. What need for more
Mutual disappointment? Shut the door.
Though now your world is cramped, dank, minuscule,
It has one denizen who has one rule:
Do what you want with your own precious time.
And there are moments, bordering on sublime
(Though these do grow less frequent, year by year)
When mind unlocks its vistas, and the sheer
Infinitude of possible combinations
That ramify in endless implications
Just opens up, and suddenly you see,
Like a man on top of a mountain near the sea.
And though these overwhelm, leaving you dizzy,
Weak-kneed, disoriented, peaked (physi-
Ologically, your lifestyle, so to speak,
Is less than ideal: every other week,
Past midnight, you sneak out to an all-night store,
Fluorescent and deserted, to get some more
Potato chips, Sprite, Ramen, frozen meals,
And cigarettes), until the whole room reels,
You tell yourself it's worth it. And you tell
Yourself, "I could be bounded in a nutshell
And count myself the king of infinite space,"
Or simply count yourself. That's one. In place
Of everyone you have yourself to blame
For all or nothing. You barely know your name
And barely need to. You failed at something, long
Ago, you think, though who was right or wrong
Matters less and less in the blur of years
Since you took cover, shutting out your fears.
Nothing gets through that door you live behind
Where the whole world is what you have in mind.

Trajectory

Who were we, back before the whole world changed?
The person jabbering in the street alone
      Was certainly deranged.
      Now he's just on the phone.
Perhaps he's trading futures – but with whom?
Can I trade mine? Or ours? But I'm a pod,
      My palm is piloted.
Have we been saved, or Pontius Pilated?
What else beside our numbers got exchanged,
      What records pirated?
   What happened to our safety zone?
      Where there's great reckoning
        There's little room,
        Even for odd.
With all the shining dials set on zoom,
   What fave new world is beckoning?
      What artificial god
With mega-memory, who does not nod?

I can't not go along. Lord knows I've tried
To keep myself from getting up to speed
      On this text-messaged ride.
      In word, if not, indeed,
In correspondence, then at least in verse,
I've felt the antiquated urge to try. Way
      Back before we let
Happen the things that hadn't happened yet,
Who thought we'd choose vehicular suicide?
      And now, caught in the net,
   Attached, we tell ourselves we're freed.
      The crashes we don't mention.
        There's no reverse,
        No hidden byway.
Will we be masters of the universe,
   Grand techno-wizards, *Übermenschen*
      Singing "I Did It My Way"?
Or roadkill on the information highway?

The Last Book

Such things were treasured objects, long ago,
Bound in calf's leather, framed by marbled boards,
Arranged by code in capitals, prized hoards
Of variorum, quire, and folio.

But now, downloaded, Xeroxed, put on tape
To quicken the commute's redundant trip,
Whole *oeuvres* shrink onto a microchip
And, volume after volume, lose their shape.

Who'll be the very last human to hold
One of these curious relics in his hands,
And think of vanished rivers, vanished birds,

And wonder why, in distant times and lands,
We made such settings for the tales we told
And placed such binding value on our words?

II Odes and Elegies

Elegy

Another year is done
And still you're gone.

Ode

O elevated visionary thoughts,
Where are you now?

For a Season

Somehow the pieces clicked at the right time,
Triumph fed triumph, and we won it all.
We were the state-of-the-art invincible
Until the fall. And did we fall.

For the Old Women

Where are they gone, the old women bent double,
The ancient woman across the alley, who tended
The peach tree, a huge wool hat in all weathers
At a right angle? Or the muddled old crone
Next door, frail but persistent, who kept stealing
My garbage cans, thinking I was throwing them out?

Under the earth like an old mother.

To False Spring

You've tricked the flowers out
  So now they die.

These are the signs
Of deity as premature arrival,
  These are the lies.

On a Porcelain Bowl

Faux Oriental blue, your figures faded,
Your legend blurred (what ritual?), and still
You're warm with what's been kept in you (coins, pins).
Surely there's truth in that. (And beauty, too.)

To a House Sparrow

Drab avatar of all that's ordinary,
Dull-uniformed, monotonous in song
    (If it *is* song),
Low-flying, mostly hopping along the ground,
You're not immortal or incomparable
But still my heart aches in a minor key
    For what you are.

On Lethargy

Too tired to write, to read, to anything!
Prisoners of heat indices, we drowse.
The chair is easy, leaving it is hard
And naps in sequence like the Florida Keys
Stretch off across the summer ...

Love, ambition, poetry ask so much
And we are so sleepy ...

For an Apple Tree

The landlord's murdered you. Your trunk's been bored,
Riddled with holes for poison, and now your leaves
Are brown as dust in August. Dying in summer!
Your apples were inedible in abundance.

The birds and squirrels won't come here anymore.

That you live on in my poems is no consolation.

To the Wind

Lift all the summer's green epiphanies,
   Yellowed to rust and fire,
     And blow them away
    O Arctic, O Canadian,
Scurry them into troughs for the underworld!

Intimations

Consider why
As infants, left alone
We cry and cry,
Straining our brand new cords
As if our hovering parents were really gone.
Surely we bawl
Under the awful stress
Of terror more primal than words,
Where absence is nothingness
And presence is all.

The constellation
Of the mobile above my crib
In circulation
Seemed the perpetual sway,
As shapes and colors would twirl and dip and jib,
Of amniotic motion.
But when it stopped
All comfort was snatched away,
As if I'd been casually dropped
In a freezing ocean.

If we could see
In a mirror the wrinkled face
Of infancy,
Would we half-recognize
In bewildered creases and furrows the frightened trace
Of an old, old man?
What in heaven had we been through?
Though we were never wise,
Was there something huge we knew
For a brief span?

Our vertigo
Does, quietly, dissipate
As we cease to know
The abyss of our becoming.
Words turn the world to a tale we learn to relate,
But that's a stage.
We mumble along in error
Forgetting what's coming,
Return to original terror
Like a blank page.

For Donald Justice

(1925-2004)

The years have failed us, as you knew they would.
Your eyes have closed at last, like the great storm shutters
On the grand hotels that only you remembered,

And as Florida gets hammered coast to coast
After the tragic season of your death
("Great Leo roared"), there isn't any justice.

(You'd wince at that, I think; I know you would.)

O memories of shadows, sunken porches,
Arcades, piano lessons, and the frail
Attempts to practice culture in the suburbs,

O hints of juniper, mysterious scents,
And the soft gradual darkening of chords
That somehow summons up the Great Depression

(Those subtleties my parents would remember
Were they alive – sometimes when reading you
I almost feel I'm hearing *them* remember),

Who will recall you now? There are no more words.

For Anthony Hecht

(1923-2004)

All style and substance, elegant and grave,
Versed in the courts of wit, and the stark places
    Sought by the wounded mind,
The heart's chambers of love, and atrocity's cave,
You put us younger poets through our paces
    With terms both strict and kind,

And, teaching by example, showed us how,
In terpsichorean stanzas learned by heart
    And smooth as alabaster,
To make the ancient forms sing here and now
With *sprezzatura*'s poise concealing art
    That earned the title "master."

Can one so measured when he took the floor
With death itself, and danced that sarabande
    With breath-taking aplomb
At tempi fitted to the chilling score,
Really have stopped? The quartet halts, unmanned.
    The instruments are dumb.

The losses come in waves. They seem too much.
The birds desert their perches, the whole flock.
    Art, being art, will last,
But it's hard to believe she can proceed with such
(An old man failing, nodding off to Bach)
    Diminishment of cast.

On Rereading Some Lines of Poetry

How many years have passed since I last read
These quiet lines? It might be five, or more,
Since I last saw them on the silent page
And heard them move across it, like a stream
Deep in the woods, that underneath the sounds
Of birdcall, insect drone, and summer leaves
Jostled by casual turns of a fitful wind,
Keeps up a steady murmur. Once again
I see their even progress in long rows
Broken at intervals by sudden shifts,
As when the contours of a meditation
Are interrupted by the thought of time,
And hear their music, barely music, faint
But sure, so close to the rhythms of the mind
We almost think its movements are our own,
And its contractions and its relaxations
The beating of our hearts.

                              Though it's been years,
The gradual accents of these paragraphs
Have not been music to a deaf man's ear.
For many times, amid the clattering lines
Of other poems, stunned by the fusillade
Of all the notes played every way at once,
Or disappointed by the random jerks
And stumblings of what's merely chopped-up prose
Meandering, or bored past sympathy
By strict, mechanical rigidity,
That stiff, robotic hammering of nails,
How often has my inner ear heard you
As what I wasn't hearing. And, what's more,
How often has the mind, that learned to read
By contemplating your instructive scenes,

Trained by those early lessons, been led on
To elevated moments, when the world
With all its crass distractions falls away,
When all our faculties, in harmony,
Combine to focus on a single page,
And, scarcely breathing, silently, with joy,
We see into the life of poems.

                              Or is
This vain delusion? Perhaps. But even so,
O archetype, profound original,
How often have your lines returned to me!

Now, suddenly, my eyes upon your page,
I find myself perplexed. Who was I then,
When I first wandered through your passages
Giddy with revelation? Reading was all
In all, and I believed myself alone
Privy to all your secrets, acolyte
Attendant on secluded meanings veiled
By simple words like "deep" and "quiet" and "joy."
Those days are past. The visionary gleam
No longer flickers in between the lines.
I cannot half-create you, just perceive.
The older man must build his own abode,
As mean as a hermit's hut in the deep woods
If need be, out of what he has at hand,
Not dream the grand baronial chateaux,
"The cloud-capp'd towers, the gorgeous palaces"
That others have erected really his.
But I still hear, though in a minor key,
The muted syllables of sleights of phrase
That conjured worlds within worlds in a flash,

Lighting the secret chambers of their art,
The inner rooms and hidden vestibules
Hung with old tapestries of pastoral scenes
Cast into clear relief. And I still feel
The sublimated sense of something else,
How all our thefts and hopeless jealousies
And petty pleasures, even the cruel words
We turn on others and against ourselves,
Belie a deeper love, of all we hold
In common trust, those strange, voluminous tomes
In which all art and nature sit inscribed,
Delineated, given their proper terms,
And which inflect all that we think and say
With lush profusion of commingling sense
And prompt, even now, those vivid moments when
The mind and all its reading interfuse
To animate the living, breathing page,
And, the whole world suspended, still inform
These very words, even these very lines.

And were this all inconsequential dream,
Or were I where I could no longer take
These soft but clear impressions, written off
By time itself, marked down, as cold as stone,
It would not matter. For here you are, right now,
My friend, my closest, truest friend, whose eyes
On this page at this moment are all that's left
To me of human sympathy and hope.
I must believe you see these shadowed lines
Lead back to other lines, and understand
The heart that's faithful to its origins
Sits like an open book, for all to read
Who care to, closely, word by chosen word.

Or do the words choose us? These words chose me
And made me who I am. So let the lines
That speak most deeply to your inmost thoughts
Shine on you like the moon, and shape your soul.
Let them blow through you like the mountain winds.
And sometime, when you can, remember me
As one who loved what you love. Remember me.

Who They Were

Long years have passed, but I still grieve,
    In silence, mostly. Poems lie.
    Though we know those we love will die
We don't believe it till they leave

And leave us dropping through thin air
    Like someone who's stepped off a cliff.
    No hypothetical "as if"
Prepares for their not being there.

The ceremonies of farewell
    Force us to put a brave face on,
    To indicate we know they've gone
And gone for good. We might as well

Attend the preacher's formal words
    Of consolation, though they're hollow.
    It's good to have a script to follow
And hymns drowned by the organ's chords.

We mourn for weeks. We grieve for years.
    And long after we've left our cave
    The memory rises like a wave
And swamps us, suddenly in tears.

2

House where we all grew up, and where
  Both our beloved parents died,
  I see you now, but from outside.
Another family's living there.

Let's hope the parents know how to live
  In rituals of domestic bliss
  And give their children the warm kiss
Only a loving home can give.

We had that, and we had much more,
  Adventures, dinner table games,
  Odd pets with comical nicknames.
I fight the urge to knock on the door

And know I won't be back again.
  It's time to let the past be gone.
  With or without love, life moves on.
I start the car. It starts to rain.

3

But still those hallways, windows, rooms
    Return in dreams, and give their shape
    To gray material, fringed with crepe.
There's no need for half-acre tombs

When smaller spaces signify
    Much more than we can ever say.
    Everyone else has gone away
And left me here, I don't know why,

While faceless forces, out of control,
    Ransack the town. I hide upstairs,
    Abandoning my post. Who cares?
I do, and wake. This takes its toll

Night after night. What's left unsaid
    Finds its way out between our lips
    Through hidden puns and Freudian slips.
Uncanny, words are never dead

And have the power to concentrate
    More meaning than we first conceive.
    Their house is some place I can't leave
Where it's too late and not too late.

4

But it's too late to leave unsaid
    The wounding words that left their mark,
    Irreverence toward the patriarch,
Or cruel ingratitude. The dead,

We pray, gain some perspective on
    The terms of human frailty
    From where they are. Where that may be,
Who knows? I don't. I know they're gone

But find it comforting to hope
    Not into utter nothingness.
    An unbeliever, more or less,
I know some things beyond my scope.

O Mother, Father, think of me!
    On high in the angelic sphere
    Forgive your poor son, if you hear.
Look on him kindly, if you see.

5

The lacerations of regret
    Can traumatize our memory.
    Some things we can't change. Let them be.
And though we never quite forget

Sins of omission, selfish acts,
    Failures of character and trust,
    They loved us, and for them we must
Accept ourselves. The heart contracts

In the raw, terminal shock of loss,
    We lurch and stumble, cry and curse
    Whatever, awful, now seems worse,
But something scrubs away the dross

Over the months and years to come,
    Call it their love. The heart expands,
    The surface shines. Through perilous lands
The bewildered spirit wanders home.

6

Which isn't what it was, a place
      One somehow didn't have to earn,
      With presences to which I'd turn,
My mother's face, my father's face,

But rather a momentary frame
      Of mind, occurring anywhere.
      As golden absences, they're there.
I almost hear them say my name

And patiently start telling me
      Some story I really might have heard
      (The drift is clear, the facts are blurred)
Set back in the vanished century

That amplifies just who they were:
      Old-world yet current, wry, genteel,
      But human, loving, hurtful, real.
I think of him, I think of her

And sense I'm never quite alone,
      With traces of their company
      More present than the world we see,
And then they're gone. I'm on my own.

7

The season's swallows dip and dive,
     Skimming the surface of the world.
     The clouds command the sky, unfurled
In monstrous blooms. In overdrive

A cold wind sweeps the skittering leaves
     Mounting in corners, clotting gutters.
     Dismayed, the spirit sags and sputters.
Life's rendered now, reduced to greaves

And liquid, not by heat but cold.
     The pale light weakens day by day.
     The summer's warmth seems years away,
A shining, fictive age of gold

Far off as childhood, and less real.
     December, and the day is here.
     Another year. (Another year!)
How much we felt, when we could feel.

8

And they were children, long ago,
    As foreign as that seems to sense.
    There's photographic evidence,
Though frail, of scenes that we can't know

Except in sepia-tinted shades
    Curled at the edges, yet somehow
    Staring right at the here and now.
And something flashes as it fades

Under nostalgia's scrutiny:
    For there they are, where we can look
    At him, entranced by a picture book,
Or her, pretending to serve tea,

And glimpse the faintest, gentlest trace
    Of features we recognize for sure
    Crystallized in miniature,
The parent's face in the child's face.

9

But shut the haunted album there.
    Don't turn from page to freighted page
    To see them changing, stage by stage,
The crinkling face, the thinning hair,

Approaching the last indignities
    In photographic pantomime,
    Succumbing to the dark lord, time,
To withering, crippling illness. Please

Remember them as who they were
    When we were young, and they were strong.
    Though not enough, that lasted long.
Just think of him. And think of her.

10

High on a hill in Hollywood,
    In Richmond, city of their birth,
    His dust, her ashes return to earth.
The place is peaceful, green. That's good:

What consolation the soul can take
    From well-trimmed lawns and handsome trees
    They take. Or we do. Subtleties
Of cultivation, which we make

In urgencies of present tense
    To say the past was here, and mattered
    (Though suddenly a whole world shattered),
Make meaning where they can't make sense.

What does make sense? The lifelong goals
    Attained when the people who most care
    Are earth and smoke and rain and air?
They were the noblest, bravest souls

It's been my privilege to know.
    I'll leave it there, and recognize
    Their silent, beautiful graves: there lies
Olivia, and there lies Joe.

III Tropes

Ship of Trope

O build your ship of trope, for you will need it.

When sand from the spreading deserts erodes the monuments,
When cities are abandoned, and tribes have moved to the north,
Your ship of trope will carry what little remains.

When the things our words once named are nothing at all,
You'll need your ship of trope, for what remains.

Gum

after GW

Nyssa or Liquidambar, Eucalyptus,
Or just a gum tree, oozing the viscous, brittle
Non-crystalline guck little by glistening little,
Which, processed, serves for anything that grips us,
Handles, galoshes, bands, belts, multi-ply
Radials, insulation, leotards,
Or sweetening the pack of trading cards
As, crackling, we blast down the road on a sugar high
Until the bubble bursts, the front tires blow,
The belt snaps, and the rookie of the year
Goes bust, big time, to wind up another bum
Just hanging around the bars, an average joe
Chewed up, spit out in the sawdust and spilled beer,
Stuck on the sole of some stranger's shoe,
                                    like gum.

Touch and Go

Skirting disaster, walking a very fine line
Like the edge of a knife, steering your rickety craft
Between perils (the abstract, the literal) and more
Perils (the pat, the abstruse), then cutting away
From the current to nudge through the shallows (to someone far
Off it may seem you are now merely drifting),
One slip of attention from foundering in oblivion,
Your *Andrew* docked in sand, its dubious cargo
Just flotsam and jetsam, bobbing off or washed up
On the island of Nowhere, never received or recorded,
With no one even to say "And whose was this?",
An enterprise all risk and little reward,
Each time you pick up a pen it's touch and go,

As in circumstances every bit as dicey
And far more dire, the surgeon with his scalpels,
His clamps and threads, laboring deep in the body,
The bloody instrument precisely firm
As he slices through tissue, opening the heart
In a dark calculus, intervention over
Trauma, as the vital signs wobble and waver
In oscillation one wayward stroke could cut
Blinking into flat-line, all systems gone,
Who, hours later, thoroughly scrubbed and drained,
Must pad down the echoing corridor to speak
With the stunned family suspended in waiting,
And say with mild reassurance and no false hope
He's done the best he can, it's touch and go,

Or the sole climber still far up the mountain, caught out
By a shift in the weather, clouds closing in fast
And the safe way down too long, who inches across
The cliff-face, toe-hold by finger-hold, with the end

Just a flinch away, no belaying rope, no buddy
(What a damned fool to come up here alone, to relish
The heady challenge, then linger, blissed, on the summit,
Drinking in the unwitnessed triumph, the pure,
Cold air, the feeling of standing on top of the world),
Who must banish such slippery thoughts, and ignore, at all cost,
The gravity of his predicament,
His muscles cramping, and concentrate on only
The sheer particulars of austere terrain
And taut discipline, finger-grip, toe-grip,
Clutching the rock like his life it's touch and go,

Or Mr. Bixby, as the sun goes down,
Deciding to risk the crossing at Hat Island
To cover his partner's bungle and make the mouth,
The silence broken by the notes of the bell
And the leadsmen, "Labboard lead! Stabboard lead!"
"M-a-r-k three! ... M-a-r-k three! ... Half twain ... Quarter twain ...
    M-a-r-k twain!",
And as the steam starts whistling through the gauge cocks
He swings the big boat into invisible marks,
She clears the first reef, then the next, and in
Absolute darkness, engines cut, she drifts
With the current, right into the sudden shadow
Cast by the massive head of the island, right on it,
The water shoaler and shoaler, the cries urgent,
"Eight-and-a-half! ... E-i-g-h-t feet! ... Seven-and- a-half ...
Seven feet! ... *Six*" and the ship scrapes bottom
"*Now*, let her have it, every ounce you've got!"
Bells ringing "Put her hard down! Snatch her! Snatch her!"
As the steamer grinds into sand it's touch and go,

And so here goes, the gamble, the desperate shot,
The wing and the flailing prayer, the Hail Mary,
The all-or-nothing go-for-broke buzzer beater
Arcing toward the goal as the light comes on,
Whether the stakes are high life or survival
Or merely the status of the reputation
Even the greenest performer puts on the line
Each time he steps into the spotlit circle
Of everyone's expectations, and his own,
Knowing the higher you go the farther you fall
With the freedom of anonymity gone forever
And the specter of utter failure always present,
Even for the poet in his rented mansard,
At his hand-me-down writing desk, who blankly stares
Out the window at the world, then down at the page,
Then off in a spectacle of catatonia,
Painted into a corner and paralyzed
As the poem comes right up to a line it can't cross
(Like plagiarizing a great American classic)
And now you have to turn it one last time
As hard as you can – are you ready? – just at the point
The contract threatens to rip under the strain
It's touch and go, *touch* and that would be *go*

Paper View

It seems, at first, a rudimentary art
With simple tools (just paper, scissors, glue),
Plain objects – maybe mountains, for a start,

Gray triangles against a sky, pale blue –
In basic two-dimensional arrangements
Even a child can work his way into,

Cut, cut, paste, paste, first tentative engagements
With making things like and unlike the world,
That meet the first frustrations and estrangements –

The piece that just fell off, the edge that curled –
And the first giddy rushes of achievement
With which a new, creative self unfurled

In blissful ignorance of pain, bereavement,
Failure, betrayal, alienation, theft,
With no conception of what to conceive meant,

No rivalry with talents much more deft,
No sense that every step you take is weighted
By all the burden that the past has left

To you, "the artist," thoroughly belated
And bounced from school to school right from the start
(Was it too much too soon? should you have waited?

At what point did your task turn into Art?),
Till gradually the darker implications
Insinuate themselves, and every part

Of what you make shows certain indications
Of just how unoriginal you are,
As illustrated by your illustrations

Of archetypal images – the Star,
The Tree, the Wave – all tried but not quite true
To either art or nature (who set the bar?

You jumped, and it came clanking down on you),
And bad enough to trigger your expulsion
From the College of Collage, but though you're through

You're never finished, the disgust, repulsion,
And anger of the audience embitters
But doesn't free you, for your old compulsion

Must quit the carpers as it quits the quitters,
Letting the whole tradition clutter your work –
Picasso, Hamilton, chair caning, Schwitters,

Canned ham, *merz,* ticket stubs, a soda jerk,
Duchamp, cracked glass, a Ballantine beer can,
And, most derivative of the handiwork

Of one not one of a kind, so not the man,
A toy monkey nailed to a screen door
Entitled "Self-portrait as Paul Cézanne" –

Till every piece becomes a metaphor
For meta-art, and you, who never met
A "meta" that you weren't a sucker for,

Sporting allusion like a carcanet,
Become not all but nothing, just a fop
With all the free will of a marionette,

The Man Who Couldn't Start and Couldn't Stop,
Misguided, garbled, a museum tour
At the end of which all sense of art goes POP,

For which the only treatment (there's no cure)
Is back to basics, wiping the dirty slate,
Preparing for a script that's simple, pure

(Though it's late to start over, far too late),
Is to think "craft" not "art," think "not too fast"
Not "now's my chance," think "modest," never "great,"

And never, never think about the Past
Dizzying at its apex – the monument
That is and ends all, being built to last

Until the last to build, the man you meant
To be, adds his great seal, the shining eye
Atop the pyramid, and the ascent

Of art through all the ages touches the sky
And stands complete, NOVUS ORDO SECLORUM,
The quest stops at the caravanserai,

The inn with room for few, the ultimate forum,
Where, handshakes all around, and secret signs,
The pale initiate brotherhood sits in quorum

Feasting on dates and figs and clementines
To welcome one who's been so quintessential –
Cancel such wicked thoughts, erase these lines,

Try something distant, patient, Oriental,
Apprenticing yourself to a vagrant swami
To focus on the spare and elemental,

And, wizardry with scissors, kirigami,
Being ruled out (sharp objects are denied you),
Learn how the crimps and folds of origami

Can summon forth the fiddling child inside you
With shapes like Water Lily, Flapping Bird –
Less tortured than the twisted forms that tried you

And found you wanting, fumbling, thick, absurd –
That, "natural as nature," signify
In the beginning was not, so to speak, the word

And its untrusty sidekick, the bald lie,
But geometric patterns that spring true
As images unfold to train the eye,

Till mimicries with "kami," birch, bamboo,
Take forms that certify or guarantee
(Like the diploma you don't have, folded in two)

A product not unlike the world we see,
Touching the bases – bird, fish, waterbomb –
In the belief a frank simplicity

Can hold the mirror up to dear old Mom
In keeping with mimetic strictures found
Listed at representational.com,

Not understanding you're on shaky ground,
All ground being shaky, Nature being a mess
With no straight edges in a world not round

Where all is fractals, patterned randomness,
And figure, poor figure, something that sticks out
Like someone showing up in evening dress

(Without a clue if not without a doubt)
To a lunchtime barbecue in a trailer park,
Not seeing an elaborate roundabout

Has funneled you back to archetypes, and stark
Knee-jerk reaction's shifting, muddled aims
Have led you to, as always, miss your mark,

And still the mind keeps playing mirror games,
Whether you're riveted or utterly bored
By pinhole perspectives of the view that frames

Receding diagonals of checkerboard
Floors in the paper houses some obscure
Dutch master fashioned out of glue, pasteboard

(You saw them, where and when you can't be sure),
And paint so scientific in detail
Space opens up, and flummoxed by the lure

Of *trompe l'oeil* trickery you're back in jail,
The prison of expectations gone awry,
Seeing Art triumph where you're bound to fail,

The truth is true art lies, and you can't lie
With half the skill to make it all seem true
To even the unsuspecting passerby

At his most gullible, even to you,
And, off your medication, losing your grip,
You tell yourself there's one thing left to do

To terminate this bummer of a trip
And shut up shop, drive home the final nail,
Your *oeuvre*'s crown, a plain gray Möbius strip

That snakes around to swallow its own tail
And, representing nothing, makes an end
Without an end, so yet once more you fail,

Recycling your fool self around the bend
Back to the finish, forward to the start
But knowing, this time, what the signs portend,

Your whole life one long bungled piece of art,
No value in it, just its cost to you,
All the way to the end it breaks your heart

And as you go you pay per paper view

A Spade a Spade

It isn't in the cards: that well-worn phrase
That means to speak the truth, to call things straight,
To "tell it like it is" (though there's that "like"),
Without evasion via metaphor,
Isn't to call one's own bluff, naming the suit –
Amid the shufflings of the smoke-filled room,
The sidelong glances, the chips stacked on the baize
Like fortress castles guarding the bends in the Rhine,
The silent faces, the sharpies counting the cards,
The sleights, the false bravura, the dare, the draw –
As anything but diamonds, clubs, or hearts.

The context's farming: naming the implement,
The humble spade, as what it merely is,
And never something as mighty as a shovel.
Its written history goes back to Plutarch,
Quoting Philip on Macedonians
In the *Apophthegmata*, although there
It seems the object to which the phrase refers,
The pure, plain, unalloyed thing itself,
Isn't a spade at all, but rather a trough,
A basin, or a bowl, or even a boat,
Having been mistranslated by Erasmus
And passed, thus garbled, into general use.

It wasn't a spade. Nor was it what we've made it
In parlance English and Americans share,
The sign of honesty, of common sense,
Of virtue, purposed, Puritanical,
Suspicious of language itself, its tricks, its lies,
Its twists of filigree and fol-de-rol
And *double entendres* that seem, well, far too French,
And threaten to sinuously undermine

A Spade a Spade

Those manly qualities we praise and prize
Above all others, founding our civics on
The solid sense our words say what we mean
And nothing else, transparent, under control,
Which helps us keep our faces utterly straight,
Our postures rigid, and our upper lips
As stiff as the starched, pressed shirts our leaders wear
As, adults among children, we steer the world.

Far from it. In Plutarch, the Macedonian king
Is telling a visitor his countrymen
Are clownish, rude, uncultured, simple-minded,
In his words, "grosse, clubbyshe, and rusticall,"
Dour, lumpish folk, "they whiche had not the witte
To call a spade by any other name"
(That's Udall, from Erasmus, with the error).
No mark of virtue, then, insistence on
A literal, stark world of denotation
Stripped of all textured resonance, all art,
All turns and colorings of metaphor,
Is rather the sign of a crude stupidity,
Unlettered, mean, suspicious, knuckle-headed,
Incapable of connecting like to like,
Of piecing the world together with the mind,
Of seeing the cream in the surf, the spokes in the dawn.

A spade a spade. A horse a horse. A lark –
You get the picture. (Or, perhaps, you don't.)
But the next time you hear a poet praised
For simple language, and a stripped-down style
Pared clean of all adornment, honest and pure,
For "plain American cats and dogs can read,"
Remember Plutarch's Philip, and ask yourself

If this is really the art that conceals art,
The master's renunciation of his craft,
Its mirror games, its metamorphoses,
Its parabolic sweeps of hyperbole,
Or merely the token of imbecility,
And ask, also, whether the critic who claims
This artless art as art's true apogee
Knows anything at all, beyond the dark
Resentments motivating bitter minds
That hate all ornament, all flair, all play,
And, caught at a literal loss by irony,
Lash out in fear the joke might be on them,
Insistent words be unambiguous,
Which isn't in the cards, and furious
That someone else is having a good time.

Nautical Terms

Not all that long ago,
We were nautical folk: barges and sloops,
    Clippers and steamers and sharpies,
Were how we got wherever we had to go,
      Moved goods and troops
    Or fled Virgilian harpies,
As if all destinations were the slips
    Where we could dock our ships.

    That's changed, of course: sports car
And jumbo jet, r. v. and high-speed train,
    Aiming at stations, lots,
And carpeted ports, carry us near and far
      Through wind and rain
    To plush vacation spots
That proffer heated pools and personal trainers.
    Now ships are for containers.

But as we moved on we
Carried the signs of our sea-faring phases
    Embedded in language itself.
We glide like shadows miles above the sea,
      But common phrases
    Accrete like an ocean shelf,
Layer on layer, sedimental, slow,
    To tell more than we know.

For did we *know the ropes*,
We'd hear the echoes of maritime concerns
Haunting the current cline,
Like sextants, compasses, and telescopes
Guiding our turns
Of phrase: we *toe the line*,
End up *over the barrel*, or get *dressed down*
Lest we screw up and drown.

Old senses linger, whether
We're stuck *in the doldrums* like a floating jail
Or *buoyed up*. We say,
Without much thought, that we're *under the weather*.
Dark skies prevail,
Then there's *the devil to pay*:
Like waves, old moods well up and *overwhelm*
The logic *at the helm*.

Then, to escape our funk,
We *tie one on*, and, *three sheets to the wind*,
We wind up *in the head*
Or *over the rail*, *groggy*, falling-down drunk.
We're caught, we're ginned
(We'd be better off dead)
Between the devil and the deep blue sea,
Footloose, not fancy free.

Since cautionary tales
Abound, like perils, on the salty freeway,
    The sea's our strategic crib.
No great shakes? Take the wind out of his sails.
        He warrants *leeway?*
    Noting *the cut of his jib*
We *give a wide berth* to the *son of a gun*,
    With room to *cut and run.*

Though context, *by and large,*
Has *gone by the board*, language doesn't *start*
    Over with a clean slate.
Words get *pressed into service*, with a charge
        That's worlds apart.
    At *the bitter end* it's late,
We've garbled it all, not knowing, our *logbooks* shut,
    The linguistic *scuttlebutt.*

How many years before
Our most precise locutions, our most fine
    Inflections and gradations
Of subtle sense, mean nothing anymore,
        Dead on the line?
    What unforeseen mutations
Will wrench our phrases, context overthrown,
    Particulars unknown?

A cautionary tale:
Like Corinth, Babylon, and Jericho
        Splintered to shards and scraps,
So too such terms. They're terminal. Detail
            Will blur and go.
        Philologists, perhaps,
Will piece together something of the past
        We were, who did not last.

        Way back when we were young
We clambered up the rigging. At full sail,
        We flew. Who could misread,
Or "the mysmetre for defaute of tonge"?
            How could words fail?
        They're all we have, indeed.
We had not sung so surely had we known
        They'd soon be on their own.

IV Odes

To an Aldabran Tortoise, Dead at 250

The races of the swift,
Who swiftly come and go
Like fads or pop stars, trending out of sight
Almost before we see them, given their gift
For getting something right
For fifteen minutes or so,
The one-hit wonders, overnight sensations,
Pet Rocks and Salad Shooters,
Or former latest software innovations
For Pleistocene computers,

Seem briefer next to you,
Known as "the only one,"
Adwaitya, oldest sentient thing alive
By eighty years or more, a tortoise who
Was once the pet of Clive
Of India. That sun
Set eons since, through veils of saffron dye
And wafture of a fan,
And while you cast a cold chelonian eye
On many a vanished man.

(Not least that lapsed grandee,
The prototypical
Nabob and potentate, big gun for hire
To profit the East India Company,
That junkie, thief, and liar
Who "owned" you, whose steep fall,
Spectacularly public, stunned the nation,
Who did confess, when tried,
Astonishment at his own moderation,
Ending a suicide.)

Now you, whose lifespan spanned
    Mozart and Bird and Cage,
Wordsworth and Motherwell, Turner and Kees,
Plus Kean and Keaton, Kierkegaard and Rand,
    Forests of old-growth trees,
    The whole Industrial Age,
Isms galore, old worlds and new world orders,
    Epochs and epistemes,
Innumerable maps redrawing borders
    For botched colonial schemes,

    Antediluvian,
    Lugging your great domed shell
For centuries, have crossed the finish line
Alone, one of a kind. Small things began
    Your terminal decline:
    For months you'd not been well;
A crack in your armor festered, gnawed by rats;
    Your liver failed; you, too,
Succumbed to time, with no more caveats,
    Dead at the Alipore Zoo.

    Still your trajectory,
    From coralline atoll
To editorial encomia
Upon your death, implies a larger story,
    Of how you came to be a
    Star of sorts, in the role
Of figure for time itself, through silent, sheer
    Endurance of life's stages
On a vast, sidereal scale, year after year
    Bridging the distant ages.

To an Aldabran Tortoise, Dead at 250

We fight, we cry, we laugh:
You turn your head and blink
And we are gone. Or were. For now you are
No longer our living, breathing chronograph,
Or Vishnu's avatar
(The second one, I think),
"Kurma," the tortoise, sent to earth to plumb
The bottom of the ocean
For what we've lost. The cold depths. Cthonic. Dumb.
A whole world in slow motion.

To Amaryllis

Cold Amaryllis, don't think I've forgotten,
After so many years and so many loves,
The cunning words, let fly with barely a shrug,
    That slit my chest wide

Open, slicing my self-esteem to little
Pieces. It's funny, the things we remember
So precisely, and how the kindnesses of
    Other women, more

Recent, more sincere, settle in silence, while
Your casual cruelties, tossed off in a
Moment some twenty years ago, still echo
    As if just spoken.

Your skilled intonations of calculated
Indifference – yes, our affair was over,
And, well, no, you hadn't told me, it wasn't
    Important enough

To bother – were masterful, I'll admit, and,
Like the work of a true artist, made to last.
I have to admire the transferential ease
    With which you transformed

Your resentment of the other to my self-
Hatred. That put an end to things, once and for
All, as you intended, except for this, a
    Belated complaint

To Amaryllis

Which doubtless will never reach you to hurt you
Who are aging now, childless and embittered,
And have forgotten we were ever in love
        If we ever were.

To the Republic

What have we done, who once were hailed
Protectors of humanity
And celebrated where we sailed,
Whose freedom set the ages free
To scheme what better states could be?
We're symbols of a deadlier sort,
Bullies despised for cruelty,
And I remain despairing of the port.

We should have known what war entailed.
Our fool imperial fantasy
Tried to command the world, and failed.
The consequences we now see:
Explosions of pure misery,
With half a million lives cut short
By death throes of democracy,
And I remain despairing of the port.

Where were the leaders who should have railed
Against such blatant idiocy
Before we launched this shit? They bailed.
Torture and illegality
Have turned our country's policy.
To import oil, we must export
American hypocrisy,
And I remain despairing of the port.

The winds grow violent. History
Breaks empires on the rocks, for sport.
Our sails are rent, we're lost, at sea,
And I remain despairing of the port.

To George Washington in Baltimore

"Great Washington, too, stands high aloft on his towering main-mast in Baltimore, and like one of Hercules' pillars, his column marks that point of human grandeur beyond which few mortals will go. ... But neither great Washington, nor Napoleon, nor Nelson, will answer a single hail from below, however madly invoked to befriend by their counsels the distracted decks on which they gaze; however it may be surmised, that their spirits penetrate through the thick haze of the future, and descry what shoals and what rocks must be shunned." – *Moby Dick*, xxxv

When Ishmael, perched high
On the swaying mast-head, scanned the panoptic view
Under an uneventful tropical sky
    Like a crow atop a tree,
    His drowsy weather eye
"Lost in the infinite series of the sea,"
The languid repetition, blue on blue
    As far as he could see,
    He thought of Nelson, you,

Napoleon, two set
In stone, one cast in bronze, polished and posted
On towering columns for centuries, to let
    A monumental pose,
    Stiff as an epithet
("Great Washington"), cold gravitas, impose
The elevated qualities thus boasted
    In laudatory shows,
    Feted, hurrahed, and toasted,

On future generations
(Imperial ambition, martial skill,
Brave sacrifice, the fatherhood of nations,
    Etcetera), to raise
    Our civic aspirations
With trophies that instill a thirst for praise,
Commemorations of the rock-hard will
    To triumph. Those were the days.
    And now? You stand there, still.

To George Washington in Baltimore

Napoleon can see,
Beyond the hôtels of the Place Vendôme,
The Place de la Concorde, the Tuilleries,
    The Louvre, Musée d'Orsay,
    Perhaps l'Orangerie,
The buttresses of St. Germain de Prés,
A panoply of pantile, spire, and dome
    On classical display,
    While Nelson is at home

    Watching the circus of
Buses and tourists flocking Trafalgar Square
(Like pigeons the locals hate, the yokels love),
    Surveying Whitehall to
    Big Ben looming above
Parliament and Westminster (Waterloo
Is probably occluded, even from there),
    A famous scene, but you
    Assume a lofty air

    To witness Baltimore
(*Some* national icons have all the luck)
Descend from pleasant city to dirt poor
    Urban calamity,
    And wonder ("never more")
What happened to the world you rose to see,
Displaced by the one with which you're likely stuck
    For what eternity
    Is left before you (*fuck*):

The Bromo Seltzer Tower
Minus the plastic bottle, City Hall
Unmarred by the foul smokestacks of the Power
       Plant, and these are the high-
       Lights, duller every hour,
As Federal Hill, the water, by and by
Were screened from view by architectural
       Embarrassment, the sky-
       Scrapers' obtrusive wall,

       Along, at least, with "Harble
Place," as the uninspired generic twin
Harbor pavilions are mocked in the Balmer garble
       Of English at its worst.
       Forget yourself to marble?
Would that you could. It wasn't this bad at first,
Or back in the Age of Gold (well, Hammered Tin),
       Before the bubble burst
       And the rowhouse roofs caved in.

       A century ago,
When Henry James, all sensibility,
Absorbed the American scene, he came to know
       Astonishingly soon,
       In half an hour or so
Beneath your simple pomp ("pleasant jejune"),
"A kind of mollified vivacity"
       That richly silent June,
       "A perfect felicity"

That charmed him, street by street,
This "cheerful little city of the dead"
(But "was it cheerful," or "resigned and discreet"?),
    The "door-stepped houses" rows
    Of "elegant" and "neat"
"Quiet old ladies, seated with their toes
Tucked-up on uniform footstools," prim, well-bred,
    And found such trim tableaus
    Endearing, or so he said,

    Though also, wordily wise,
He paused to register a "still small shock"
At finding "the bourgeois," and to "recognize"
    The Muse of History,
    And in her "strange deep eyes"
The shadow of the War for slavery.
You were like a "stately old-fashioned clock"
    Guarding a parlour he
    Examined to unlock

    Family secrets told
By the tone of things (furniture, *objets d'art*,
Domestic treasures bought with what we sold
    Our land for, "treasures of Style"),
    And from such manifold
Odd decorative pieces of domicile
Information, he measured who we are,
    Noticing, all the while,
    The perspectival jar

To George Washington in Baltimore

Peculiar to our nation,
Where vulgar intervals (like brownstone) cast
A lingering illusion of duration
On antecedent stages,
A temporal "consecration":
Decades turn centuries; centuries, ages;
The fairly recent "nobly antique." The past
Assembling in his pages
Was subtle. That didn't last.

If our observant guest
Were here today, he'd get a larger shock
(Not that anywhere else would pass his test).
Though ironies are rich,
We're poor in what we're best
At: gaffes of formstone; tacky sins of kitsch
Like "window art"; TV rooms crammed with schlock;
The street smack ("Fuck you bitch!");
The crack houses; the Block.

Aesthetics? Don't be absurd.
We live in a time and place where anything goes.
Would the Master entertain the Spoken Word?
Or groove on 98
Rock? High-five the Bird?
Exquisitely expert, concatenate
The history of taste with *Pink Flamingoes*?
Deign to participate
In workshops? Pick up lingoes?

He would, above it all,
See you still there, observing all along
With lidless eyes, cool, imperturbable,
Constantly unsuspended,
But not uncomical:
If glanced at from a certain unintended
Perspective, something's hilariously wrong,
As your right arm, extended,
Seems an enormous dong

(Made longer by your right
Hand's grip on a sheaf of paper – more of that),
"The father of our country pose," a sight
The Master did not see
Or did not mention. Quite
Embarrassing, even for you, to be
So flagrantly exposed to seamy, scat-
Ologic ribaldry,
Though you, of course, don't bat

An eye, being inured
To the slings and arrows public figures come
To count on from the public, which can't be cured
Of bouts of ritual
Abuse, and resting assured
Your rigid pose, stiffly mechanical
(That arm, held out forever, must be numb),
Is vastly preferable
To something really dumb:

The original design
Envisioned you decked out in Roman dress,
Steering a horse-drawn chariot, in line
      With conventional depictions
      Of Power, palatine,
Timelessly sovereign, shaped by the fictions
We fashion to memorially impress,
      Oblivious of restrictions
      Like the financial distress

      Of rampant overrun
That led the overseers to scrap that plan –
A scaled-down tribute being better than none
      Given shrinking resources –
      And choose what could be done
Sans balconies, sans chariot, sans horses,
And closer to the essence of the man.
      (Reality enforces.
      We do the best we can.)

      Thus you stand dressed as normal
(Overcoat, trousers, wig), holding that sheaf
In a gesture somehow casual yet formal
      (That half-detached position,
      Nuanced, seemed to inform all
"Great Washington" did), finished with your mission
To free the states for good, in plain relief
      Resigning your commission
      As first Commander in Chief,

Just like the man himself
(As if he saw what might be from your tower,
Sensing the rocks, the shoals, the hidden shelf,
  The slaughtering of factions
  Like Ghibelline and Guelph,
The bloody, Thermidorian reactions
Of vicious states) took, in his finest hour,
  That most rare of actions
  And gave up all his power.

  Let Napoleon have
Paris (where he's been up and down, to say
The least, considered a hero or a knave
  As each republic lists
  In accents sometimes grave,
Sometimes acute, given to leftist twists
Or rightist turns depending who holds sway,
  Toppled by royalists
  And by Gustave Courbet,

  Who fled to beat the rap,
A crippling fine), and let Lord Nelson keep
London beneath his gaze, athwart his cap-
  Stan in an action shot
  And caked in pigeon crap
Spoiling his Creigleith sandstone: you'll take your lot
And stay in Baltimore (write it and weep)
  To stand for what they're not
  On heights where the fall is steep.

(And let that holy fool,
Saint Simeon Stylites, keep his post
As pioneer of the ascetic school
  And connoisseur of pain,
  His body but a tool
That frost, heat, hail, damp, sleet, and wind, and rain
Compete, year in, year out, to punish most
  For spiritual gain,
  And gory is the host

  With maggots to his aid,
Hair shirts, spiked collars, flagellation, burns,
The bitter instruments of the martyr's trade,
  Whose use, however sick,
  Is how the game is played
By arts that study the next difficult trick,
Like sacrificing imagery for urns
  Of polished rhetoric
  Taking its costly turns.)

  No tyrant and no martyr,
Not covetous of an imperial crown,
Stigmata, nor the Order of the Garter,
  Steady in your good name
  You wouldn't smirch or barter
For anything, unmoved by your own fame,
I wonder what you think as you look down
  (With pride? or growing shame?)
  To your eponymous town

And its huge monument
Sleek as a rocket, one brute phallic thrust
Piercing the heavens with muscular intent,
    Its monstrous obelisk
    A pointed message sent
Without diplomacy, streamlined and brisk,
To all the little nations: "In guns we trust";
    "We call the game, it's Risk";
    "Submit"; "Empire or bust."

    "Great Washington" knew war,
Knew power, knew honor, was not for sale.
You're just a statue, true, but standing for
    A slippery ideal
    Of statecraft, civil, more
Enlightened, subject to the commonweal,
And monolithic simulacra fail,
    Grotesque, malign, unreal
    Beside your human scale.

To My Friends

My good friends, when you're under the illusion
That the common end of things has ended me,
Whether that end was sudden or wretchedly slow,
Peaceful or violent, untimely or, finally, wished for,

Don't spend too much time grieving, as if I were gone
To some murky underground region of swampy water
And cavernous absence, metallic and silent and cold,
Or some plush resort in the stratosphere of our dreams

Pillowed with cumuli, graced by ethereal muzak,
Or some massive confusing impersonal processing center
With lines and obscure snafus and numbers not names,
Away from the sun and the sound of the wind in the trees,

But after a short ceremony, public or private,
Listen for the wings of the birds, and ask where we're going,
Alabama or Delaware, Canada, Yucatán,
And wish me luck in the next life, who now have wings.

Index of Titles and First Lines

A Note About the Author

Joseph Harrison was born in Richmond, Virginia, grew up in Virginia and Alabama, and studied at Yale and Johns Hopkins. His book *Someone Else's Name* (Waywiser, 2003) was named as one of five poetry books of the year by the *Washington Post* and was a finalist for the Poets' Prize. His poems have appeared in *The Best American Poetry 1998* (ed. John Hollander), *180 More Extraordinary Poems for Every Day* (ed. Billy Collins), The Library of America's *Anthology of American Religious Poems* (ed. Harold Bloom), and many journals. In 2005 he was the recipient of an Academy Award in Literature from the American Academy of Arts and Letters. He lives in Baltimore.

Other books from Waywiser

*Expanded UK edition